AF689144

Cash-Eater Crickets

Cash-Eater Crickets

Matthew Petchinsky

1

Cash-Eater Crickets: How Insects Predict Economic Collapse

By: Matthew Petchinsky

DISCLAIMER

This book, *Cash-Eater Crickets: How Insects Predict Economic Collapse*, is a speculative, analytical, and metaphorical work intended for **educational, illustrative, and conceptual purposes only**. It does **not** constitute financial advice, investment advice, economic forecasting services, professional consulting, or recommendations of any kind. The author is not a licensed financial advisor, economist, accountant, broker, or legal professional, and nothing within this book should be interpreted as a substitute for advice from qualified professionals.

The concepts, models, narratives, and symbolic frameworks presented in this book—particularly those involving insects, biological behavior, ecological systems, and their relationship to economic patterns—are **metaphorical, analogical, and interpretive** in nature. While references may be made to real-world economic events, historical patterns, market behaviors, inflationary cycles, supply chain disruptions, or financial systems, these references are used **solely to explore ideas and thought experiments**, not to predict, guarantee, or declare future outcomes.

Any discussion of economic collapse, financial instability, currency devaluation, debt cycles, market failures, or systemic risk is **not a prediction, warning, or prophecy**, but an exploration of how human systems may be interpreted through symbolic, ecological, and behavioral lenses. Economic conditions are influenced by countless variables beyond the scope of this book, and no outcomes described herein should be relied upon for personal, business, or institutional decision-making.

This book does **not** encourage fear-based financial behavior, panic selling, hoarding, market withdrawal, or distrust of institutions. Readers are solely responsible for their financial choices and actions. Past events, hypothetical scenarios, or illustrative case studies discussed in this work do not guarantee future performance or results.

References to insects, crickets, or biological systems—whether literal or symbolic—are **not presented as scientific proof or empirical forecasting tools**. Any biological comparisons are used for **conceptual insight, pattern recognition, and narrative clarity**, not as validated economic indicators. No claims are made that insects can literally predict markets, crashes, or financial events.

This work may include **creative language, speculative analysis, symbolic interpretation, and unconventional frameworks** designed to provoke critical thinking, awareness, and discussion. It is not intended to replace academic economic research, peer-reviewed science, or professional financial analysis.

Nothing in this book should be interpreted as a call to action, investment strategy, survival guide, or economic manifesto. The author makes no guarantees regarding accuracy, completeness, timeliness, or applicability of the information contained herein.

By reading this book, you acknowledge that you understand and accept that all material is provided **"as-is," without warranties of any kind**, express or implied. The author and publisher disclaim any liability for losses, damages, or consequences—financial or otherwise—that may arise directly or indirectly from the use, interpretation, or misinterpretation of the content.

This book is intended for **intellectual exploration, metaphorical insight, and critical reflection** only. Readers are encouraged to seek professional guidance before making any financial, economic, or legal decisions.

All rights reserved.

Introduction

Before the market crashes... the bugs come. Here's how to listen.

Long before charts turned red, before headlines screamed panic, before analysts scrambled to explain what had already happened, **something else always moved first**.

Not traders.
Not governments.
Not algorithms.

The insects.

Crickets in particular.

Across ancient civilizations, agricultural societies, and pre-industrial economies, unusual insect behavior was never ignored. Sudden swarms, mass disappearances, erratic chirring cycles, migrations that broke seasonal rules—these were not curiosities. They were warnings. Signals that the ground beneath human systems was shifting.

Modern finance dismissed these signs as superstition. Markets became abstract, digital, detached from soil, seasons, and biology. We replaced natural indicators with spreadsheets, derivatives, and predictive models built on assumptions of perpetual growth.

And yet—again and again—markets collapse **after** the insects change.

This book exists in the space where those two worlds collide.

Cash-Eater Crickets is not about mysticism disguised as economics, nor economics stripped of reality. It is about **pattern recognition across systems**. It explores how biological stress signals—especially among insects with short lifecycles and extreme environmental sensitivity—often precede economic instability, liquidity crises, and collective human panic.

Crickets thrive, migrate, fall silent, or devour resources when ecosystems destabilize. Markets do the same.

Both respond first to pressure.
Both react before language forms.
Both tell the truth long before institutions admit it.

By blending ancient entomological observation with modern financial theory, behavioral economics, and systemic risk analysis, this book teaches you how to **read early signals**—not to predict exact dates or numbers, but to recognize *when conditions are no longer stable*. When noise replaces rhythm. When consumption turns frantic. When survival behavior overrides balance.

This is not a book about fear.
It is a book about **attention**.

Because by the time markets speak, it's already too late.

The insects never wait.

Chapter 1: The Chirp Index – When Crickets Get Loud

Markets do not collapse quietly.

They vibrate first.

Before numbers fall, **rhythm breaks**. Volatility does not arrive as a single event; it announces itself through increasing noise, repetition, and urgency. Traders feel it as agitation. Consumers feel it as restlessness. Ecosystems feel it as stress.

Crickets feel it first.

The Biology of Loudness

Crickets chirp for specific reasons: mating, territory, temperature regulation, and survival signaling. Under stable environmental conditions, their chirps follow predictable cycles—steady rhythms tied to temperature, daylight, and season. Entomologists have long used cricket chirps as natural thermometers, not because crickets "predict" temperature, but because their bodies **respond immediately to environmental shifts**.

When conditions destabilize—heat spikes, food scarcity, atmospheric pressure changes, electromagnetic interference—chirp frequency changes. It becomes louder. Faster. More erratic. Sometimes it doesn't stop at all.

This is not confidence.

It is strain.

Crickets chirp louder when the system they rely on can no longer regulate itself quietly.

Noise as a Precursor to Collapse

Financial markets behave the same way.

Before crashes, markets get loud:

- News cycles accelerate
- Opinions multiply
- Experts contradict each other hourly
- Price movements become exaggerated
- Minor events trigger outsized reactions

This is the market chirping.

The **Chirp Index** is not a literal measurement, but a framework: when a system produces excessive signal to compensate for instability, collapse becomes statistically more likely. Loudness increases when control weakens.

Healthy systems don't need to shout.

Crickets and Capital

Crickets increase output when:

- Resources feel threatened
- Competition intensifies
- Environmental predictability collapses
- Survival windows shorten

Markets do the same when:

- Liquidity tightens
- Debt burdens rise
- Growth narratives fracture
- Time horizons compress

The louder the market gets—socially, emotionally, informationally—the more it resembles a stressed ecosystem.

This is why market tops often feel euphoric, chaotic, and over-communicated. Everything is "breaking news." Every move is framed as historic. Every voice demands attention.

Silence would reveal weakness.

Noise hides it—temporarily.

False Confidence Is a Survival Signal

In crickets, loudness is often misread as dominance. In reality, it's frequently a sign of **exposure**. The louder the chirp, the greater the energy expenditure. The greater the energy expenditure, the lower the margin for error.

Markets at peak loudness behave the same way. They burn capital, attention, leverage, and credibility faster than they replenish them.

This is why collapses feel sudden—but were not.

The system was screaming long before it broke.

Reading the Chirp Index in Human Systems

You are not listening for volume alone. You are listening for **pattern changes**:

- Repetition without progress
- Explanations replacing results
- Narratives looping instead of evolving
- Urgency replacing clarity

When a market can no longer move quietly, it compensates with sound.

That is the chirp.

And when chirping becomes constant, the environment is no longer stable enough to support it.

The First Signal Is Always Behavioral

Crickets do not predict collapse.

They respond to it **forming**.

Markets do not fall because of one event.

They fall because the underlying rhythm breaks.

The Chirp Index teaches you to recognize when sound replaces structure—when volume replaces value.

Once you hear it, you can't unhear it.

Journal Prompts

1. Where in your financial life does noise currently outweigh clarity?
2. What headlines or narratives feel repetitive rather than informative?
3. When have you mistaken excitement or urgency for stability in the past?
4. What systems in your life get louder when they are under stress?
5. Where are you expending energy to maintain appearances rather than foundations?
6. What does "quiet confidence" look like in your finances?
7. When do you personally get louder—emotionally or mentally—under pressure?
8. Which voices do you listen to more when uncertainty increases, and why?
9. What signals are you ignoring because they don't shout?
10. How would your decisions change if you valued rhythm over noise?

Closing Reflection

Crickets don't scream because they are winning.

They scream because the ground is shifting.

When systems lose balance, they compensate with sound. Markets do it. Media does it. People do it.

The Chirp Index is not about predicting the exact moment of collapse—it is about recognizing **when silence is gone**. When rhythm fractures. When noise becomes necessary to hold the system together.

By the time everything is loud, the collapse is already rehearsing.

Learning to listen is not about fear.

It is about timing.

Chapter 2: Swarm Economics – When Survival Replaces Strategy

Markets do not fail because people suddenly become irrational.

They fail because **survival thinking spreads faster than logic**.

In nature, a swarm is not chaos—it is coordination under stress. When food becomes scarce, environments shift rapidly, or threats multiply, insects abandon individuality. Strategy collapses into instinct. Efficiency gives way to speed. The goal is no longer optimization, but **continuity**.

This is the moment when economics stops behaving like a long-term system and starts behaving like an organism under attack.

The Biology of the Swarm

Insects swarm when three conditions align:

- Resource pressure increases
- Environmental signals conflict or destabilize
- Time horizons shorten dramatically

A cricket alone chirps. A swarm moves.

Swarming is not planned. There is no central intelligence issuing commands. Each insect responds to micro-signals from its neighbors—movement, vibration, density. Once a critical threshold is reached, individual decision-making vanishes. The swarm becomes the decision.

This is not mass hysteria.

It is **distributed survival intelligence**.

Markets Under Swarm Pressure

Financial markets enter swarm mode under strikingly similar conditions:

- Liquidity becomes uncertain
- Narratives fracture and multiply
- Long-term planning feels unsafe
- Short-term preservation dominates behavior

Investors stop asking, "What is this worth?"
They start asking, "What is everyone else doing?"

This is the exact moment strategy dies.

Swarm economics replaces fundamentals with momentum, fundamentals with fear, and analysis with imitation. Buying and selling no longer reflect belief—they reflect proximity.

From Herd Mentality to Swarm Dynamics

The term "herd behavior" understates what actually happens. Herds move slowly. Swarms move instantly.

In a swarm:

- Small movements cause massive cascades
- False signals amplify faster than true ones
- Direction matters less than participation
- Standing still feels fatal

This is why markets overshoot—upward and downward. Swarm dynamics do not stop at balance. They exhaust the environment.

Crickets devour everything not because they are greedy, but because **waiting equals death**.

Why Swarms Always Consume Too Much

Insects in swarms do not ration. They cannot assume tomorrow exists.

Markets in swarm mode do the same:

- Capital is over-leveraged
- Risk is underpriced
- Gains are chased without exits
- Losses trigger stampedes

This is where bubbles are born and crashes become unavoidable. Systems optimized for efficiency cannot survive when every participant switches to survival mode simultaneously.

The swarm does not collapse the system.

The system collapses because it **can no longer support swarming behavior**.

Social Media: The Artificial Swarm Accelerator

Modern markets swarm faster than any biological system in history.

Why?

Because humans have built digital pheromones.

Likes, shares, trending topics, algorithmic amplification—these are not neutral tools. They replicate the chemical signals insects use to coordinate swarms. The result is a market that reacts not to reality, but to **perceived density of belief**.

The louder the signal, the more real it feels.

Accuracy becomes irrelevant.

Speed becomes everything.

When You Feel the Swarm Inside You

The most dangerous part of swarm economics is not what it does to markets.

It's what it does to you.

You will notice:

- Urgency replacing patience
- Anxiety when you're not "in"
- Relief when you follow the crowd
- Fear of missing movement more than fear of loss

This is not weakness.

It is biology.

Recognizing swarm activation in yourself is the earliest personal warning signal that systemic stability is deteriorating.

The Exit Problem

In swarms, exits do not exist.

Once you are inside, movement options collapse. The density becomes the trap. This is why most participants experience crashes not as events, but as **sudden realizations**: "I can't get out."

Crickets cannot stop swarming mid-flight.

Markets cannot de-leverage instantly.

By the time survival replaces strategy, the window has already narrowed.

Journal Prompts

1. When have you made financial decisions primarily based on what others were doing?
2. What emotions arise when you feel “left behind” financially?
3. Where in your life does speed override reflection?
4. How do you personally react when uncertainty spikes—freeze, follow, or flee?
5. What signals make you feel urgency even without clear information?
6. When have you confused movement with progress?
7. What would slowing down feel like during moments of financial pressure?
8. Where are you currently operating in survival mode rather than strategic mode?
9. What systems in your life reward swarming behavior?
10. How could you design more personal “exits” before pressure rises?

Closing Reflection

Swarms are not mistakes.

They are nature’s response to environments that no longer support patience.

When markets swarm, it is not because people are foolish—it is because the system has trained them to survive faster than they can think. The danger is not joining the swarm.

The danger is forgetting that it is one.

Once you learn to recognize when survival replaces strategy, you gain something rare in unstable systems:

The ability to pause while everything else rushes.

And in collapsing environments, pause is power.

Chapter 3: Ant Colonies and Asset Patterns

Ant colonies never collapse because one ant makes a bad decision.

They collapse when **patterns stop distributing risk**.

Ants are among the most successful economic organisms on Earth. They store resources, diversify labor, build redundant infrastructure, and survive environmental shocks that wipe out larger species. They do this without markets, without currency, and without central planners.

Yet even ant colonies fail.

When they do, the failure is not sudden. It is structural.

This chapter explores how ant colony behavior reveals deep truths about asset distribution, concentration, and systemic fragility—and why modern economies ignore these lessons at their peril.

The Architecture of the Colony

An ant colony is not a hierarchy. It is a network.

No single ant understands the whole system. Each ant follows simple rules:

- Gather when resources are available
- Store across multiple chambers
- Repair continuously
- Adapt roles based on need
- Abandon paths that no longer yield returns

This is not intelligence as humans define it.

It is **pattern-based resilience**.

Colonies survive because assets—food, labor, risk—are distributed rather than centralized.

Asset Distribution as Survival Strategy

Healthy colonies do not store everything in one place.

They spread food caches across chambers with different temperature, humidity, and access points. Some stores will fail. That is expected. Redundancy is not waste—it is protection.

Modern financial systems claim to understand diversification.

In practice, they do the opposite.

Assets become concentrated:

- Capital pools into a few institutions
- Risk is bundled into opaque instruments
- Supply chains optimize for efficiency, not resilience
- Wealth accumulates faster than it circulates

This looks productive—until stress arrives.

When Optimization Becomes Fragility

Ant colonies fail when they over-optimize.

Research shows colonies collapse when:

- Too much food is stored in one chamber
- Foraging paths become rigid
- Ant roles stop rotating
- Feedback signals are ignored

These failures mirror economic collapses exactly.

Markets optimized for speed and profit sacrifice adaptability. The moment conditions change, the system cannot reroute fast enough. The colony does not starve because food vanished—it starves because **food cannot reach where it's needed**.

This is not scarcity.

It is misallocation.

Asset Patterns Tell the Truth First

Ants read patterns, not prices.
They respond to:

- Flow interruptions
- Traffic congestion
- Resource decay
- Structural bottlenecks

Markets reveal instability through similar signals:

- Liquidity freezes
- Supply chain delays
- Capital hoarding
- Asset bubbles detached from use-value

When assets stop moving naturally, something is wrong—even if balance sheets still look strong.

This is why crashes feel shocking to those watching numbers, but obvious to those watching **movement**.

The Illusion of Central Control

There is no "ant CEO."

Colonies function because no single node carries the system. When economies centralize control—financially, politically, or technologically—they remove the very redundancy that allows survival.

When one institution becomes "too big to fail," the colony is already in danger.

Ant colonies do not bail out failing chambers.

They abandon them.

What Ants Teach About Personal Assets

This lesson applies beyond markets.
Personal financial collapse often mirrors colony failure:

- Income depends on one source
- Savings live in one account
- Skills are too specialized
- Time is over-leveraged

Resilience is not about having more.
It is about **having spread**.
Ants survive because no single loss ends the colony.

Journal Prompts

1. Where are your financial resources overly concentrated?
2. What assets in your life move easily—and which are stuck?
3. How many of your systems depend on a single point of failure?
4. Where have you optimized for efficiency at the expense of flexibility?
5. What redundancy do you currently view as "waste"?
6. When have you ignored small disruptions that later became crises?
7. How diversified are your skills, not just your money?
8. What would it mean to distribute risk more evenly in your life?
9. Where are you relying on control instead of adaptability?
10. What systems would survive if one major component failed?

Closing Reflection

Ant colonies do not collapse because they lack resources.

They collapse because their **patterns break**.

When assets stop flowing, when storage becomes rigid, when risk concentrates instead of disperses, the system becomes fragile—no matter how large it appears.

Markets fall the same way.

Not from emptiness.

From imbalance.

Watching ant colonies teaches a crucial truth: survival does not belong to the biggest, the richest, or the fastest.

It belongs to the most **distributed**.

Chapter 4: Beetles in the Blockchain – The Scarab Logic of Digital Value

Not all wealth moves forward.

Some wealth must be **rolled, sealed, and preserved**—or it rots.

Long before blockchains, before ledgers, before coinage itself, ancient civilizations watched beetles and understood something modern finance is only beginning to relearn: value survives not through speed, but through **cycle integrity**.

The Egyptian dung beetle—the scarab—was not worshipped by accident.

It was observed.

The Scarab as the First Ledger

To the ancient Egyptians, the scarab was a living equation.

Each day, the beetle rolled a ball of dung across the ground, shaping it carefully, sealing nutrients inside, burying it, and returning later to harvest what had transformed within. From decay came continuity. From waste came future life.

This was not symbolism imposed after the fact.

It was **economic observation**.

The scarab demonstrated four principles that underpin all durable value systems:

1. Collection of raw input (waste, surplus, chaos)
2. Compression into a discrete unit
3. Secure storage through time
4. Delayed extraction of value

That is a blockchain.

Why Dung Matters

Dung is excess. It is what remains after consumption.
In economic terms, dung represents:

- Transaction byproducts
- Fees
- Energy expenditure
- Information exhaust
- Surplus data

The scarab does not ignore waste.
It **turns it into currency**.

Modern economies produce vast amounts of informational dung—data, transactions, micro-movements of capital. Blockchain technology emerged not to create value from nothing, but to **capture, verify, and preserve the residue of economic activity**.

Just as the scarab shapes dung into a standardized sphere, blockchains compress chaotic activity into discrete, verifiable blocks.

Rolling Value Through Time

The scarab rolls its dung ball forward, not randomly, but persistently—often against terrain, gravity, and predators. The effort is immense relative to its size.

This mirrors digital asset systems that require energy, computation, and redundancy to maintain integrity. Proof-of-work, proof-of-stake, and distributed consensus are not inefficiencies.

They are **friction as protection**.

Systems that move value too easily invite corruption.

The scarab understands this instinctively.

Burial as Security

Once formed, the dung ball is buried.

Hidden.

Removed from immediate access.

This is not hoarding—it is **time-locking**.

In ancient Egyptian belief, the scarab symbolized rebirth because burial was not an end. It was a delay mechanism. Transformation required darkness, pressure, and patience.

Blockchains operate similarly:

- Assets are locked in smart contracts
- Transactions are irreversible
- Records cannot be altered without consensus
- Time becomes a security feature

The scarab teaches that value exposed too long degrades.

Value protected through time matures.

Decentralization Without Consciousness

No scarab controls the system.

No beetle governs the desert.

Yet across generations, the behavior persists with astonishing consistency. This is decentralized order without central authority—a principle blockchains attempt to recreate digitally.

When systems rely on trust in individuals, they fail.

When systems rely on **repeatable behavior encoded into structure**, they endure.

The scarab does not need faith.

It needs function.

When Scarab Systems Fail

Even scarab systems collapse when cycles break.
If:

- Waste becomes toxic
- Soil becomes hostile
- Time horizons shorten
- Predators overwhelm the process

Then the beetle's labor fails.
Blockchain systems fail under similar conditions:

- When energy costs exceed value stored
- When speculation replaces utility
- When centralization creeps back in
- When speed overrides verification

The lesson is not that the system is flawed.
The lesson is that **cycles must be respected**.

Personal Scarab Economics

This logic applies to your life.
What do you do with your excess?

- Time
- Energy
- Money
- Attention
- Experience

Do you discard it?
Or do you shape it, secure it, and allow it to mature?
Short-term consumption destroys value.
Cyclic preservation creates it.

Journal Prompts

1. What “waste” in your life could be transformed into future value?
2. Where do you rush value instead of allowing it to mature?
3. What systems do you trust too much because they feel fast or easy?
4. Where could friction actually protect you?
5. What assets in your life need to be time-locked?
6. How do you currently store your effort across time?
7. What cycles do you keep breaking prematurely?
8. Where have you confused visibility with security?
9. How could decentralization improve resilience in your life?
10. What would it mean to treat value as something grown, not grabbed?

Closing Reflection

The scarab does not create wealth.

It **completes the cycle**.

Modern markets obsess over creation—new assets, new tokens, new growth—while ignoring preservation, verification, and patience. The Egyptian dung beetle reminds us that value is not what shines first.

It is what survives burial.

Blockchains did not invent this truth.

They rediscovered it—written long ago in sand, soil, and beetle tracks.

And like all ancient lessons, it only works if we listen.

Chapter 5: Preying Mantis = Predatory Loans

The most dangerous predators do not chase.

They wait.

The preying mantis survives not through speed, strength, or numbers, but through **stillness disguised as safety**. It does not announce danger. It does not signal aggression. It looks calm. Balanced. Even benevolent.

Until it strikes.

Predatory lending works the same way.

This chapter examines how the behavior of the preying mantis mirrors financial systems that profit not from growth, but from **entrapment**, and why these systems thrive most when people are stressed, distracted, or desperate.

The Biology of the Ambush

A preying mantis does not hunt randomly. It positions itself where prey already wants to go—near flowers, light, warmth, or shelter. It blends into familiarity. Its posture is deceptive: upright, almost prayerful, as if harmless.

The strike is instantaneous.

There is no warning because warning would reduce effectiveness.

Predatory loans follow identical logic:

- They appear during moments of need
- They present as solutions, not threats
- They emphasize relief, not cost
- They hide the mechanism of capture

The danger is not force.

The danger is **timing**.

Why Predators Target the Vulnerable

Mantises do not attack the strongest insects.
They target those already exposed:

- Injured
- Distracted
- Isolated
- Low on energy

Predatory lenders do the same:

- Medical emergencies
- Housing instability
- Job loss
- Credit damage
- Emotional exhaustion

These systems are not accidents of capitalism.
They are **adaptive predators**.
They evolve to exploit stress conditions created elsewhere in the ecosystem.

The Illusion of Choice

A mantis does not chase prey across open ground.
It waits until the prey moves *into range*.
Predatory financial products operate by shrinking perceived options:

- "This is your only approval"
- "No credit check"
- "Instant cash"
- "Flexible payments"

Choice exists in theory, not in practice.
When options collapse, consent becomes mechanical.
This is not free-market interaction.
It is **coerced proximity**.

Interest as Consumption

When a mantis feeds, it does not kill instantly.

It consumes slowly.

Predatory loans function the same way. The principal is rarely the profit. The profit is time—interest accumulated through prolonged dependence.

The borrower is not meant to escape quickly.

They are meant to remain alive enough to keep paying.

This is not service.

It is **harvesting**.

Why Escape Is So Difficult

Insect prey caught by a mantis often continues moving even after capture. The nervous system lags behind reality.

Borrowers experience the same phenomenon:

- Payments continue even when balance grows
- Hope persists despite worsening terms
- Identity shifts from "user" to "trapped"

The system relies on **delay between awareness and action**.

By the time the truth is felt, leverage is gone.

Predators Thrive in Silent Systems

Mantises hunt alone.
Predatory loans thrive in isolation:

- Shame prevents disclosure
- Complexity prevents understanding
- Speed prevents reflection
- Silence prevents resistance

The system does not need to win arguments.
It needs you not to speak.

Breaking the Predatory Pattern

In nature, mantises are controlled by:

- Environmental disruption
- Increased visibility
- Collective movement
- Early detection

Financial predators collapse under the same conditions.

Awareness is not enough.

Pattern recognition is required.

Once you see the ambush posture, the stillness stops looking peaceful.

Journal Prompts

1. Where in your life have "easy solutions" come with hidden costs?
2. When have you accepted terms because you felt you had no alternatives?
3. What financial decisions were made during stress rather than clarity?
4. Where does speed prevent you from fully understanding consequences?
5. What systems profit from your prolonged dependence?
6. How does shame affect your financial communication?
7. What warning signs did you notice only after commitment?
8. Where could slowing down protect you from future harm?
9. Who could you involve earlier to avoid isolation-based decisions?
10. What would true financial safety feel like—without urgency?

Closing Reflection

The preying mantis is not evil.

It is efficient.

Predatory loans are not personal attacks.

They are systems optimized for extraction under pressure.

Understanding this removes shame and restores agency.

Once you recognize that danger does not always rush—but often waits quietly—you gain the most powerful defense available in any ecosystem:

The ability to step out of range.

Predators cannot strike what refuses proximity.

And the first act of financial freedom is learning when stillness is not peace—but a warning.

Chapter 6: Building the Insect Investment Network

Insects do not survive alone.

Even the most solitary species depends on networks—hidden, overlapping systems of signals, resources, and shared environments that allow adaptation faster than any individual could manage. No insect attempts to dominate the ecosystem. Instead, survival emerges from **interconnection, redundancy, and responsiveness**.

This is the model modern investors have forgotten.

The goal of an insect investment network is not prediction.

It is **resilience**.

Why Singular Strategies Fail

Human financial systems often worship singularity:

- One income stream
- One winning asset
- One platform
- One timing strategy
- One "right" answer

Insects never do this.

No colony relies on one food source. No swarm depends on one path. No beetle trusts one burial site. Networks form because environments change faster than certainty.

Singular strategies feel efficient—until they snap.

Insect logic assumes instability as the default.

The Network Principle

An insect investment network is built on five principles:

1. **Distributed Inputs** – Information, resources, and signals come from multiple, unrelated sources
2. **Low Dependency Nodes** – No single asset or strategy is essential for survival
3. **Fast Signal Recognition** – Early warnings matter more than precise forecasts
4. **Role Fluidity** – Assets change function depending on conditions
5. **Energy Awareness** – Systems never consume more energy than they can replace

This is not diversification for profit.
This is diversification for **continuity**.

Signals Over Predictions

Insects do not forecast seasons mathematically.

They respond to:

- Temperature shifts
- Humidity changes
- Chemical traces
- Behavioral deviations in other species

Your financial network should do the same.

Instead of asking:

"Where will the market be next year?"

You ask:

- Where is liquidity slowing?
- Where is noise increasing?
- Where is leverage hiding?
- Where is behavior changing before numbers do?

The network does not need certainty.

It needs **early discomfort**.

Asset Roles, Not Asset Identities

Insect systems assign roles dynamically.

A tunnel used for storage becomes an escape route during floods. A forager becomes a defender when threats rise. Value is not fixed—it is contextual.

Assets work the same way:

- Cash becomes safety, then opportunity
- Skills become income, then leverage
- Time becomes learning, then positioning
- Information becomes awareness, then restraint

An insect investment network asks:

"What does this asset do *now*?"

Not:

"What was this asset designed for?"

Avoiding Overconnection

Insects avoid one critical mistake humans make: **total synchronization**.

Too much connection creates cascade failure.

Ant colonies isolate chambers. Swarms split when density becomes dangerous. Beetles distribute burial sites.

Your network must include **intentional disconnection**:

- Assets that do not move together
- Information sources outside consensus
- Strategies that benefit from stillness
- Reserves untouched by daily volatility

Resilience requires separation.

Building Your Personal Insect Network

This network includes:

- Financial assets (cash, stores of value, low-volatility buffers)
- Skill assets (adaptable, transferable abilities)
- Social assets (non-extractive relationships)
- Time assets (uncommitted attention)
- Informational assets (pattern-based awareness, not hype)

Each node must be small enough to fail without destroying the system.

Insects expect loss.

That expectation is what keeps them alive.

The Final Shift: From Winning to Surviving Well

Markets teach domination.

Insects teach endurance.

An insect investment network does not aim to beat the system. It aims to **outlast instability**, preserve optionality, and remain mobile while others freeze.

When collapse arrives, insects do not panic.

They reroute.

Journal Prompts

1. Where is your financial life overly dependent on a single outcome?
2. What assets or skills could fail without destroying your stability?
3. Which signals do you notice before numbers change?
4. Where are you overconnected to consensus thinking?
5. What resources do you currently protect from daily volatility?
6. How flexible are your assets when conditions shift?
7. What would resilience look like without growth pressure?
8. Where could intentional disconnection increase safety?
9. What small losses could you accept to prevent catastrophic ones?
10. How would your decisions change if survival—not winning—was the goal?

Closing Reflection

Insects do not build empires.

They build systems that endure fires, floods, winters, and collapse.

The insect investment network is not glamorous. It will never feel impressive in boom times. But when systems strain, liquidity tightens, and noise overwhelms clarity, it does something far more valuable than winning:

It keeps you moving.

Resilience is not passive.

It is **designed**.

And once built, it listens long before markets scream.

Appendix A: The Q1–Q4 Bug Signal Tracker (With Financial Alerts)

This appendix is designed as a **practical decoding tool**, not a prediction engine. The Bug Signal Tracker does not tell you *what will happen*. It tells you **when systems are becoming biologically and behaviorally unstable**—often before markets acknowledge it.

Insects respond first because they cannot lie to themselves.

Humans and markets can.

Use this tracker as a **seasonal awareness map**, aligning biological stress signals with recurring financial behaviors across the calendar year. The goal is not timing perfection, but **early recognition and adaptive posture**.

How to Use the Bug Signal Tracker

Each quarter includes:

- **Primary Insect Signal**
- **Observed Biological Behavior**
- **Market Behavior Parallel**
- **Financial Alert Level**
- **Recommended Posture**
- **Questions to Ask Before Acting**

You are not meant to react to a single signal.
You are meant to notice **clusters**.

One insect changing behavior is noise.
Many insects shifting patterns is a warning.

Q1 (January–March): Dormancy Stress & False Stability

Primary Bug Signal

Crickets, ants, and beetles show **delayed emergence**, erratic activity bursts, or premature movement during cold periods.

Biological Pattern

- Dormant insects awaken too early
- Activity spikes followed by sudden stillness
- Resource probing without commitment
- Energy conservation mixed with confusion

This indicates **environmental mismatch**—conditions appear safe but are not yet stable.

Market Parallel

- "New year optimism" masking unresolved structural issues
- Rallies driven by narrative, not fundamentals
- Institutions rebalancing quietly
- Retail confidence returning too quickly

Financial Alert Level

◈ Caution Alert – False Calm

What This Means

The system wants to believe stability has returned, but underlying stress remains unresolved. Markets may rise, but movement lacks conviction.

Recommended Posture

- Observe more than act
- Reduce leverage
- Avoid chasing early-year rallies
- Build liquidity buffers

Questions to Ask

- Is this movement driven by repair—or hope?
- What problems were "reset," not solved?
- Who benefits most from early optimism?

Q2 (April–June): Expansion Pressure & Overforaging

Primary Bug Signal
Ant colonies overextend foraging paths; crickets increase chirp frequency; beetles increase resource rolling.

Biological Pattern

- Aggressive expansion
- Increased energy expenditure
- Risk-taking behavior
- Reduced redundancy

This is **growth under pressure**, not abundance.

Market Parallel

- Capital floods into risk assets
- New products, tokens, and opportunities multiply
- Credit expands
- Speculation increases

Financial Alert Level

⟐ Instability Alert – Overextension

What This Means

Growth is real—but fragile. Systems are stretching faster than resilience can support.

Recommended Posture

- Take partial profits
- Rebalance toward resilience
- Reduce exposure to hype-driven assets
- Strengthen non-correlated positions

Questions to Ask

- What is growing faster than it can be sustained?
- Where is risk being disguised as innovation?
- What happens if momentum stalls?

Q3 (July–September): Heat Stress & Consumption Frenzy

Primary Bug Signal

Swarming behavior, aggressive feeding, increased predation, and visible die-offs among weaker insects.

Biological Pattern

- Survival replaces efficiency
- Consumption accelerates
- Cooperation weakens
- Error rates increase

This is **environmental overheating**.

Market Parallel

- Volatility spikes
- Liquidity thins
- Sudden reversals become common
- Debt stress surfaces
- Retail panic begins

Financial Alert Level

◈ High Risk Alert – Structural Strain

What This Means

The system is no longer optimizing—it is enduring. This is where crashes often begin forming, even if they don't finalize yet.

Recommended Posture

- Preserve capital
- Avoid new long-term commitments
- Increase defensive positions
- Protect optionality

Questions to Ask

- Where is desperation replacing strategy?
- Which assets rely on constant inflows to survive?
- Who is being forced to sell?

Q4 (October–December): Collapse, Consolidation, or Reset

Primary Bug Signal

Mass die-offs, migration, deep burrowing, hoarding behavior, or total silence.

Biological Pattern

- Systems shut down excess activity
- Resources are locked away
- Only core survival behaviors remain
- Weak systems fail completely

This is **truth season**.

Market Parallel

- Crashes, corrections, or forced reckonings
- Institutional consolidation
- Tax-loss harvesting
- Narrative rewriting
- "No one saw it coming" headlines

Financial Alert Level

⟐ Critical Alert – System Resolution

What This Means

Whatever could not survive stress is removed. This is not chaos—it is sorting.

Recommended Posture

- Do not panic
- Look for post-collapse clarity
- Prepare for redeployment—not immediately, but deliberately
- Preserve psychological calm

Questions to Ask

- What survived without intervention?
- What failed despite support?
- Where is silence returning?

Cross-Quarter Warning Signals (Immediate Alerts)

If you observe **any three** of the following simultaneously, treat it as an **override alert**, regardless of quarter:

- Excessive media noise without substance
- Sudden regulatory changes
- Explosive growth in low-quality assets
- Rapid credit tightening
- Public disbelief in obvious stress
- Normalization of emergency language

◈ **Override Alert: Systemic Risk Rising**

Personal Use Tracker (Optional Practice)
At the end of each month, record:

- Market noise level (1–10)
- Personal stress level (1–10)
- Observed urgency in decision-making
- Assets that feel "too loud"
- Areas of silence or stillness

Patterns matter more than numbers.

Closing Reflection
Insects do not need quarterly reports.

They feel instability as vibration, heat, pressure, and scarcity—and they act accordingly.

Markets collapse when humans ignore the same signals.

The Bug Signal Tracker is not about fear. It is about **alignment with reality before narrative catches up**. When you learn to listen across quarters instead of reacting to headlines, you stop being surprised by outcomes others call sudden.

The insects always knew.

Now you do too.

Message from the Author:

I hope you enjoyed this book, I love astrology and knew there was not a book such as this out on the shelf. I love metaphysical items as well. Please check out my other books:

-Life of Government Benefits

-My life of Hell

-My life with Hydrocephalus

-Red Sky

-World Domination:Woman's rule

-World Domination:Woman's Rule 2: The War

-Life and Banishment of Apophis: book 1

-The Kidney Friendly Diet

-The Ultimate Hemp Cookbook

-Creating a Dispensary(legally)

-Cleanliness throughout life: the importance of showering from childhood to adulthood.

-Strong Roots: The Risks of Overcoddling children

-Hemp Horoscopes: Cosmic Insights and Earthly Healing

- Celestial Hemp Navigating the Zodiac: Through the Green Cosmos

-Astrological Hemp: Aligning The Stars with Earth's Ancient Herb

-The Astrological Guide to Hemp: Stars, Signs, and Sacred Leaves

-Green Growth: Innovative Marketing Strategies for your Hemp Products and Dispensary

-Cosmic Cannabis

-Astrological Munchies

-Henry The Hemp

-Zodiacal Roots: The Astrological Soul Of Hemp

- **Green Constellations: Intersection of Hemp and Zodiac**

-Hemp in The Houses: An astrological Adventure Through The Cannabis Galaxy

-Galactic Ganja Guide

Heavenly Hemp
Zodiac Leaves
Doctor Who Astrology
Cannastrology
Stellar Satvias and Cosmic Indicas
Celestial Cannabis: A Zodiac Journey
AstroHerbology: The Sky and The Soil: Volume 1
AstroHerbology:Celestial Cannabis:Volume 2
Cosmic Cannabis Cultivation
The Starry Guide to Herbal Harmony: Volume 1
The Starry Guide to Herbal Harmony: Cannabis Universe: Volume 2
Yugioh Astrology: Astrological Guide to Deck, Duels and more
Nightmare Mansion: Echoes of The Abyss
Nightmare Mansion 2: Legacy of Shadows
Nightmare Mansion 3: Shadows of the Forgotten
Nightmare Mansion 4: Echoes of the Damned
The Life and Banishment of Apophis: Book 2
Nightmare Mansion: Halls of Despair
Healing with Herb: Cannabis and Hydrocephalus
Planetary Pot: Aligning with Astrological Herbs: Volume 1
Fast Track to Freedom: 30 Days to Financial Independence Using AI, Assets, and Agile Hustles
Cosmic Hemp Pathways
How to Become Financially Free in 30 Days: 10,000 Paths to Prosperity
Zodiacal Herbage: Astrological Insights: Volume 1
Nightmare Mansion: Whispers in the Walls
The Daleks Invade Atlantis
Henry the hemp and Hydrocephalus

10X The Kidney Friendly Diet
Cannabis Universe: Adult coloring book

Hemp Astrology: The Healing Power of the Stars

Zodiacal Herbage: Astrological Insights: Cannabis Universe: Volume 2

Planetary Pot: Aligning with Astrological Herbs: Cannabis Universes: Volume 2

Doctor Who: Convergence Protocol – The Replicator War

Nightmare Mansion: Curse of the Blood Moon

The Celestial Stoner: A Guide to the Zodiac

Cosmic Pleasures: Sex Toy Astrology for Every Sign

Hydrocephalus Astrology: Navigating the Stars and Healing Waters

Lapis and the Mischievous Chocolate Bar

Celestial Positions: Sexual Astrology for Every Sign

Apophis's Shadow Work Journal: **:** A Journey of Self-Discovery and Healing

Kinky Cosmos: Sexual Kink Astrology for Every Sign

Digital Cosmos: The Astrological Digimon Compendium

Stellar Seeds: The Cosmic Guide to Growing with Astrology

Apophis's Daily Gratitude Journal

Cat Astrology: Feline Mysteries of the Cosmos

The Cosmic Kama Sutra: An Astrological Guide to Sexual Positions

Unleash Your Potential: A Guided Journal Powered by AI Insights

Whispers of the Enchanted Grove

Cosmic Pleasures: An Astrological Guide to Sexual Kinks

369, 12 Manifestation Journal

Whisper of the nocturne journal(blank journal for writing or drawing)

The Boogey Book

Locked In Reflection: A Chastity Journey Through Locktober

Generating Wealth Quickly:How to Generate $100,000 in 24 Hours

Star Magic: Harness the Power of the Universe

The Flatulence Chronicles: A Fart Journal for Self-Discovery

The Doctor and The Death Moth

Seize the Day: A Personal Seizure Tracking Journal

The Ultimate Boogeyman Safari: A Journey into the Boogie World and Beyond

Whispers of Samhain: 1,000 Spells of Love, Luck, and Lunar Magic: Samhain Spell Book

Apophis's guides:Witch's Spellbook Crafting Guide for Halloween

Frost & Flame: The Enchanted Yule Grimoire of 1000 Winter Spells

The Ultimate Boogey Goo Guide & Spooky Activities for Halloween Fun

Harmony of the Scales: A Libra's Spellcraft for Balance and Beauty

The Enchanted Advent: 36 Days of Christmas Wonders

Nightmare Mansion: The Labyrinth of Screams

Harvest of Enchantment: 1,000 Spells of Gratitude, Love, and Fortune for Thanksgiving

The Boogey Chronicles: A Journal of Nightly Encounters and Shadowy Secrets

The 12 Days of Financial Freedom: A Step-by-Step Christmas Countdown to Transform Your Finances

Sigil of the Eternal Spiral Blank Journal

A Christmas Feast: Timeless Recipes for Every Meal

Holiday Stress-Free Solutions: A Survival Guide to Thriving During the Festive Season

Yu-Gi-Oh! Holiday Gifting Mastery: The Ultimate Guide for Fans and Newcomers Alike

Holiday Harmony: A Hydrocephalus Survival Guide for the Festive Season

Celestial Craft: The Witch's Almanac for 2025 – A Cosmic Guide to Manifestations, Moons, and Mystical Events

Doctor Who: The Toymaker's Winter Wonderland

Tulsa King Unveiled: A Thrilling Guide to Stallone's Mafia Masterpiece

Pendulum Craft: A Complete Guide to Crafting and Using Personalized Divination Tools

Nightmare Mansion: Santa's Eternal Eve

Starlight Noel: A Cosmic Journey through Christmas Mysteries

The Dark Architect: Unlocking the Blueprint of Existence

Surviving the Embrace: The Ultimate Guide to Encounters with The Hugging Molly

The Enchanted Codex: Secrets of the Craft for Witches, Wiccans, and Pagans

Harvest of Gratitude: A Complete Thanksgiving Guide

Yuletide Essentials: A Complete Guide to an Authentic and Magical Christmas

Celestial Smokes: A Cosmic Guide to Cigars and Astrology

Living in Balance: A Comprehensive Survival Guide to Thriving with Diabetes Insipidus

Cosmic Symbiosis: The Venom Zodiac Chronicles

The Cursed Paw of Ambition

Cosmic Symbiosis: The Astrological Venom Journal

Celestial Wonders Unfold: A Stargazer's Guide to the Cosmos (2024-2029)

The Ultimate Black Friday Prepper's Guide: Mastering Shopping Strategies and Savings

Cosmic Sales: The Astrological Guide to Black Friday Shopping

Legends of the Corn Mother and Other Harvest Myths

Whispers of the Harvest: The Corn Mother's Journal

The Evergreen Spellbook

The Doctor Meets the Boogeyman

The White Witch of Rose Hall's SpellBook

The Gingerbread Golem's Shadow: A Study in Sweet Darkness

The Gingerbread Golem Codex: An Academic Exploration of Sweet Myths

The Gingerbread Golem Grimoire: Sweet Magicks and Spells for the Festive Witch

The Curse of the Gingerbread Golem

10-minute Christmas Crafts for kids

Christmas Crisis Solutions: The Ultimate Last-Minute Survival Guide

Gingerbread Golem Recipes: Holiday Treats with a Magical Twist

The Infinite Key: Unlocking Mystical Secrets of the Ages

Enchanted Yule: A Wiccan and Pagan Guide to a Magical and Memorable Season

Dinosaurs of Power: Unlocking Ancient Magick

Astro-Dinos: The Cosmic Guide to Prehistoric Wisdom

Gallifrey's Yule Logs: A Festive Doctor Who Cookbook

The Dino Grimoire: Secrets of Prehistoric Magick

The Gift They Never Knew They Needed

The Gingerbread Golem's Culinary Alchemy: Enchanting Recipes for a Sweetly Dark Feast

A Time Lord Christmas: Holiday Adventures with the Doctor

Krampusproofing Your Home: Defensive Strategies for Yule

Silent Frights: A Collection of Christmas Creepypastas to Chill Your Bones

Santa Raptor's Jolly Carnage: A Dino-Claus Christmas Tale

Prehistoric Palettes: A Dino Wicca Coloring Journey

The Christmas Wishkeeper Chronicles

The Starlight Sleigh: A Holiday Journey

Elf Secrets: The True Magic of the North Pole

Candy Cane Conjurations

Cooking with Kids: Recipes Under 20 Minutes

Doctor Who: The TARDIS Confiscation

The Anxiety First Aid Kit: Quick Tools to Calm Your Mind

Frosty Whispers: A Winter's Tale

The Infinite Key: Unlocking the Secrets to Prosperity, Resilience, and Purpose

The Grasping Void: Why You'll Regret This Purchase

Astrology for Busy Bees: Star Signs Simplified

The Instant Focus Formula: Cut Through the Noise

The Secret Language of Colors: Unlocking the Emotional Codes

Sacred Fossil Chronicles: Blank Journal

The Christmas Cottage Miracle

Feeding Frenzy: Graboid-Inspired Recipes

Manifest in Minutes: The Quick Law of Attraction Guide

The Symbiote Chronicles: Doctor Who's Venomous Journey

Think Tiny, Grow Big: The Minimalist Mindset

The Energy Key: Unlocking Limitless Motivation

New Year, New Magic: Manifesting Your Best Year Yet

Unstoppable You: Mastering Confidence in Minutes

Infinite Energy: The Secret to Never Feeling Drained

Lightning Focus: Mastering the Art of Productivity in a Distracted World

Saturnalia Manifestation Magick: A Guide to Unlocking Abundance During the Solstice

Graboids and Garland: The Ultimate Tremors-Themed Christmas Guide

12 Nights of Holiday Magic

The Power of Pause: 60-Second Mindfulness Practices

The Quick Reset: How to Reclaim Your Life After Burnout

The Shadow Eater: A Tale of Despair and Survival

The Micro-Mastery Method: Transform Your Skills in Just Minutes a Day

Reclaiming Time: How to Live More by Doing Less

Chronovore: The Eternal Nexus

The Mind Reset: Unlocking Your Inner Peace in a Chaotic World
Confidence Code: Building Unshakable Self-Belief
Baby the Vampire Terrier
Baby the Vampire Terrier's Christmas Adventure
Celestial Streams: The Content Creator's Astrology Manual
The Wealth Whisperer: Unlocking Abundance with Everyday Actions
The Energy Equation: Maximize Your Output Without Burning Out
The Happiness Algorithm: Science-Backed Steps to Joyful Living
Stress-Free Success: Achieving Goals Without Anxiety
Mindful Wealth: The New Blueprint for Financial Freedom
The Festive Flavors of New Year: A Culinary Celebration
The Master's Gambit: Keys of Eternal Power
Shadowed Secrets: Groundhog Day Mysteries
Beneath the Burrow: Lessons from the Groundhog
Spring's Whispers: The Groundhog's Prediction
The Limitless Mindset: Unlock Your Untapped Potential
The Focus Funnel: How to Cut Through Chaos and Get Results
Bold Moves: Building Courage to Live on Your Terms
The Daily Shift: Simple Practices for Lasting Transformation
The Quarter-Life Reset: Thriving in Your 20s and 30s
The Art of Shadowplay: Building Your Own Personal Myth
The Eternal Loop: Finding Purpose in Repetition
Burrowing Wisdom: Life Lessons from the Groundhog
Shadow Work: A Groundhog Day Perspective
Love in Bloom: 5-Minute Romantic Gestures
The Shadowspell Codex: Secrets of Forbidden Magick
The Burnout Cure: Finding Balance in a Busy World
The Groundhog Prophecy: Unlocking Seasonal Secrets
Nog Tales: The Spirited History of Eggnog
Six More Weeks: Embracing Seasonal Transitions
The Lumivian Chronicles: Fragments of the Fifth Dimension

Money on Your Mind: A Beginner's Guide to Wealth
The Focus Fix: Breaking Through Distraction
January's Spirit Keepers: Mystical Protectors of the Cold
Creativity Unchained: Unlocking Your Wildest Ideas in 2025
Manifestation Mastery: 365 Days to Rewrite Your Reality
The Groundhog's Mirror: Reflecting on Change
The Weeping Angels' Christmas Curse
Burrowed in Time: A Groundhog Day Journey
Heartbeats: Poems to Share with Your Valentine
Dino Wicca: The Sacred Grimoire of Prehistoric Magick
Courage of the Pride: Finding Your Inner Roar
The Lion's Leap: Bold Moves for Big Results
Healthy Hustle: Achieving Without Overworking
Practical Manifesting: Turning Dreams into Reality in 2025
Jurassic Pharaohs: Unlocking the Magick of Ancient Egypt and Dino Wicca
The Happiness Equation: Small Changes for Big Joy
The Confidence Compass: Finding Your Inner Strength
Whispers in the Hollow: Tales of the Forgotten Beasts
Echoes from the Hollow: The Return of Forgotten Beasts
The Hollow Ascendant: The Rise of the Forgotten Beasts
The Relationship Reset: Building Better Connections
Mastering the Morning: How to Win the Day Before 8 AM
The Shadow's Dance: Groundhog Day Symbolism
Cupid's Kitchen: Quick Valentine's Day Recipes
Valentine's Day on a Budget: Love Without Breaking the Bank
Astrocraft: Aligning the Stars in the World of Minecraft
Forecasting Life: Groundhog Day Reflections
Bleeding Hearts: Twisted Tales of Valentine's Terror
Herbal Smoke Revolution: The Ultimate Guide to Nature's Cigarette Alternative

Winter's Wrath: The Complete Survival Blueprint for Extreme Freezes.

The Groundhog's Shadow: A Tale of Seasons
Burrowed Insights: Wisdom from the Groundhog
Sensual Strings: The Art of Erotic Bondage
Whispered Flames: Unlocking the Power of Fire Play
Forgotten Shadows: A Guide to Cryptids Lost to Time
Six Weeks of Secrets: Groundhog Day's Hidden Messages
Shadows and Cycles: Groundhog Day Reflections
The Art of Love Letters: Crafting the Perfect Message
Romantic Getaways at Home: Turning Your Space into Paradise
Purrfect Brews: A Cat Lover's Guide to Coffee and Companionship
The Groundhog's Wisdom: Timeless Lessons for Modern Life
The Shadow Oracle: Groundhog Day as a Predictor
Emerging from the Burrow: A Journey of Renewal
The Language of Love: Learning Your Partner's Love Style
Authorpreneur: The Ultimate Blueprint for Writing, Publishing, and Thriving as an Author
Weathering the Seasons: Groundhog Day Perspectives
Valentine's Day Magic: A Guide to Romantic Rituals
The Shadow Chronicles: Stories of Groundhog Day
Love and Laughter: Fun Games for Valentine's Day
AstroRealty: Unlocking the Stars for Property Success
The Groundhog's Path: A Guide to Seasonal Balance
Groundhog Day Diaries: Reflections in the Shadow
The Groundhog's Light: Illuminating the Path Ahead
Valentine's Traditions from Around the World
AI Wealth Revolution: Unlocking the Trillionaire Mindset
Love Rekindled: Reigniting Passion in Relationships
Single and Thriving: Self-Love on Valentine's Day
Emerald Legends: Mystical Tales of Ireland
Green Alchemy: Harnessing Nature's Magic
The Hearts of Horror: A Valentine's Day Nightmare

The Leprechaun's Guide to Wealth and Wisdom

Dancing with the Sidhe: Celebrating the Otherworld

Shamrocks and Shadows: Mysteries of the Green Isle

Emerald Energy: Harnessing Luck and Growth

The Gingerbread Golem's Valentine: A Sweetheart's Guide to Love and Enchantment

The Celtic Knot: Weaving Life and Destiny

Green Fire: Elemental Magic for St. Patrick's Day

Clover Chronicles: Finding Your Inner Luck

Ireland's Mystical Creatures: A Field Guide

Gingerbread Golem's Love Almanac

Prowl and Thrive: The Lion's Guide to Success

Love Alchemy: Transforming Your Life Through Heart Energy

WORLD DOMINATION: Woman's Rule 3:The New Life

The Midnight Rose: A Guide to Lunar Love Spells

The Forbidden Letters: Writing Your Own Love Prophecy

Luck and Lore: St. Patrick's Day for Modern Mystics

The Green Path: A Pagan Celebration of Renewal

The Dark Architect's Guide to Reprogramming Reality

Prankster's Paradise: A Guide to Harmless Hijinks

Manifest Your Reality: The Law of Attraction Simplified

The TARDIS Owner's Manual: Understanding the Doctor's Ship: *A complete guide to the TARDIS, its technology, secrets, and mysteries*

Starlit Romance: Astrology Secrets for Finding True Love

The Time Lord's Atlas: A Complete Guide to the Whoniverse: ***A breakdown of the locations, planets, and dimensions explored in Doctor Who***

Sweetheart Shadows: The Dark Side of Love and Attraction

February Fire: Reigniting Passion in Every Area of Life

The Self-Love Toolkit: 5 Ways to Embrace Who You Are

February Sparks: Ignite Your Dreams in 28 Days

March to Success: A 31-Day Action Blueprint
Ancient Paths: The 13 Sacred Principles of Dino Wicca
Echoes of Tomorrow: Navigating the AI Revolution
The Wellness Blueprint: Balancing Mind, Body, and Soul
Green Horizons: Sustainable Living for a Better Tomorrow
The AI Wealth Code: How to Make Millions with Automation
AI-Powered Creativity: Writing, Art, and Music for Profit
Extinction Rites: Rebirthing Your Soul Through Prehistoric Magick
Sacred Serpents tarot
Celestial Enchantment blank journal
Star Strains
Culinary Journeys: Exploring Global Flavors at Home
The Hollowvale Curse
The Hollowvale Harvest
The Egg of Transformation: Awakening Your Inner Power
Blooming Into Power: A Wiccan Guide to Spring Awakening
The Nightmare Nexus: The Third Doctor's Perilous Haunting
Digital Detox: Reclaiming Your Life in a Connected World
Ostara's Path: Walking the Spiral of Renewal
The Sacred Hare
Financial Freedom: Building Wealth in the Modern Age
Spring's Cauldron: Stirring the Waters of Change
The Hollowvale Pact
Quantum Consciousness: The Science of Reality Shifting
The Hollowvale Hunger
The Sacred Waters Within: A Witch's Guide to Hydrocephalus Magick
The Raven's Nest: Building a Life of Unshakable Stability
AI and the Human Mind: The Future of Intelligence
The Hollowvale Reckoning
Timeless Love: Building and Maintaining Lasting Relationships

The Raven's Roar: Unlocking Unstoppable Confidence
Raven Sight: Awakening Intuition and Inner Wisdom
The Butterfly Effect: Small Changes, Big Transformations
Taming the Boogeyman: How to Conquer Your Inner Fears
The Magick of Green: Awakening Earth's Energy in You
The Entrepreneurial Mindset: Secrets to Business Success
The Hollowvale End
The Shadow Luck Ritual: Reclaiming Power from Your Dark Side
Spring Magick for Beginners: A Simple Guide to Seasonal Energy Work
Doctor Who: The Hollowvale Conundrum
The March of Miracles: Unlocking Synchronicities in Spring
Unveiling the Cosmos: A Guide to Stargazing and Space Exploration
The Ultimate Guide to Surviving an Economic Collapse
The AI Gold Rush: How to Profit from the AI Revolution
Bastet's Shadow: The Hidden Power of Feline Magick
The Bastet Codex: Unlocking the Goddess's Magickal Secrets
Purring Spells: Harnessing Bastet's Healing Frequencies
Bastet's Nine Lives: Rebirth, Transformation, and Immortality Spells
Primal Currents: Hydrocephalus Magick in the Path of Dino Wicca
The Digital Gold Rush: Mastering E-Commerce and Online Sales
Future Shock: Adapting to the Next Decade of Change
The Quantum Mindset: Think Like a Billionaire
Sacred Motherhood: Awakening the Divine Feminine Within
The Mother's Spellbook: Enchantments for Love, Protection, and Prosperity
The Witch's Guide to Parenting: Raising Empowered and Intuitive Children

The Magick of Motherhood: Reclaiming Your Power Through Rituals
The Pagan Path to Self-Love: A Goddess's Guide to Worth and Confidence
Wild Woman Magick: Unleashing Your Primal Power
The Money Magnet Blueprint: Unlocking Unlimited Wealth
Biohacking 101: Unlock Your Body's Full Potential
The Wild Father: A Pagan Guide to Strength and Wisdom
The Sacred Masculine: Unlocking Your Inner Power
The Druid's Compass
The Warrior's Mindset
The Father's Fire
Odin's Path
Ancestral Bonds
The House That Whispers
The Magician's Code
The Wild Hunt
The Green Man's Path
The Altar of Success
The Shadow and the Sword
The High Priestess's Guide to Energy Healing
The Lunar Mother
The Sacred Self-Care Grimoire
The Womb Wisdom Codex
The Wheel of the Mother
The Witch's Guide to Manifestation
The Q2 Reset
The Ultimate Guide to AI-Powered Passive Income
Escape the 9-5
AI Feline Fortunes
The Tear-Stained Grimoire
Razorblade Runes
Cemetery Sirens

The Midnight Wristwatch
The Town That Forgets
AI Horror & Creepypasta
The Hollow Frequency
The Breach Echo
The Quiet Between Worlds
The Sigil of Tharan-Khul
Summon the Vault of Y'ha'ten
The Becoming Codex
The Profit of Az'ra-nar
The Drowned Logos
Echoes of the Eldritch Will
The Deep Ledger
Necronomicon of Networth
Covenant of the Wealthwyrm
The Whisperer's Manifesto
The Rites of Azh-K'luth
The Ark of the Crawling Coin
The Tithe of Shadows
Inkheart Abyss
The Timewinds of Y'ha-nthlei
The Spiral Labyrinth of Azag-Nirrh
The Gallifreyan Heresy of the Black Pharaoh
The Psalms of Nyog-Sotha
Black Rain Alchemy
The Infinite Maw
The Entropic Blueprint
The Oracle of Sh'guul
The Book of Breach
The Drowned Saint's Testament
Dreamcraft of the Sleeper God
The Silence Market
Cthonomics: The Dark Wealth Algorithm

Invocation of the Ten-Eyed King
Wealthbound to the Wyrm Below
Become the Unnameable
Codex of the Sovereign Flame
Rituals of Relentless Becoming
The Shadow Ascends
The Eyes Beneath You
The Will That Wakes Worlds
Silence Is a Weapon
The Mirror That Screams
The Whisper Between Moments
The Mind That Devours Fear
The Myth of the Finished Self
The Architect of Your Madness
The Voice You've Buried
The Discipline of Madness
Stormborn: Awakening Your Inner Tempest
The Mind That Ate Time
Unbind Your Becoming
The Pact You Owe Yourself
The Devourer's Diet
The Acid That Carves the Path
The Tower You Must Burn
The Breath Between Worlds
Speak Like the Deep
The Labyrinth Within
The Spine of the Sea God
Rejection Is a Portal
The Crown You Refused
The Scar Is the Spell
The Lightless Flame
The Habit of Becoming Horrific
ChickenJockey Chaos

The Gatekeeper Within
You Are Not Your Name
The Compass of the Mad
The Archive of Unsent Letters
What the Mirror Can't Show You
The Knife You Needed
Worship Nothing, Become Everything
The Other Voice
The Body the World Forgot
The Vein of the Void
The Black Bone Codex
The Puzzle of the Hidden Self (Millennium Puzzle)
The Eye That Sees the Lie *(Millennium Eye)*
The Ring of Return (Millennium Ring)
The Rod of Relentless Will *(Millennium Rod)*
The Tally of the Soul (Millennium Tauk/Necklace)
The Key to the Locked Timeline (Millennium Key)
The Scale of Sacred Decisions (Millennium Scales)
Inferno Bites: The UnOfficial Minecraft Lava Cookbook
Rot in the Attic
Prana: The Hidden Force of Your Infinite Self
The Shadow Realm Within: Transforming Darkness Into Destiny
The Borderland Collapse
Claws of Protection: Bastet's Defensive Magick
Mr. Ring-a-Ding's Madness
Yugioh Astrology: Celestial Deckcraft and Duel Destiny (2026–2027 Edition)
The Seal You Signed: Unlocking the Power You Once Feared
The Puzzle of Infinite Minds: Unlocking the Mentalism Hidden Within
The Eye That Mirrors the All: Secrets of Inner Reflection
Doctor Who: The Toymaker's Broadcast

Rootwake: The Carbon Covenant

Skitter Logic: Unlearning the Fear That Built You

Doctor Who: The World That Froths

Rootwake: The Fizz That Rewrites Flesh

Rootwake: Frothfather of the World

The Holly Pact: Blood Beneath the Mistletoe

The 2nd Mass Principle: Building Unbreakable Tribes

Web of Wits: A Survival Guide to Encounters with Anasi the Spider (Aunt Nancy)

The Hexbreaking Handbook: Effective Spells to Remove Curses

Pop Alchemy: Transform Your Life One Sip at a Time

The Mason Code: Leading in Unleadable Times

Petosiris and the Fifth Chamber of Thoth

The Ether Seed Within

The Parent of Tomorrow

Petosiris's Pyramid of Perpetual Wealth

Unlearn the World

Grimoire of the Hollow Tongue

Zodiac Weeds: Finding Your Strain Through the Stars

Aquarius Rises in the Bank

The Sugar God's Smile

The Skinclock Reversal: Biohacking the Face of Time

Debtburn: How to Obliterate What You Owe Forever

The Ice Cream Oracle: What Your Cone Says About Your Future

Silence Is Sovereignty: The Power of Being Unreadable

The Wind That Whispers Through Stone

Path of the Four Directions

Doctor Who: The Maestro's Symphony of Endings

Oxygen Grail: Breathing to Undo the Clock

Zodiacal Collapse: When Stars Devour Time

Teachings from the Red Sand Silence

Doctor Who: Omega – The Broken Equation
Memory Wipe Your Past: Start Over Like a MiB
Mitochondria Prime: Ignite the Core of Youth
A Nest of Roaches
Grub from the Galaxy: MiB Recipes You'll Never Forget
Whiskers of Power: Bastet's Guide to Inner Sovereignty
The Gift Must Cost Them: Negotiation Through Unequal Exchange
The Worm Guys' Wealth Code: Hustle Like an Alien
Bug Out: The Edgar Method for Ruthless Goal Setting
Weaving Life with Spiderwoman's Pattern
Doctor Who: The Rani's Renaissance
How to Get a Job (If You're a Puppygirl)
Speak Through Others: The Art of Proxy Power
T-Rex Your Trauma: Reclaim the Power of Your Primal Self
The Black Briefcase: How MiB Stay Wealthy in Silence
The Thirst Beyond Reason: Understanding Diabetes Insipidus From the Inside Out
Backwoods Witchcraft for Billionaires: The Pagan Path from Dirt Roads to Gold Roads
The Moonshine Grimoire: Fermented Spells for Abundance
The Nameless Geometry
The Wraith's Mixtape: Spellcasting with Songs of Sorrow
The Gallifreyan Gentleman: Silent Wealth, Sonic Confidence, and the Doctor's Code of Living
Sugar Water Confidence
Dino Totems: Spirit Guides from Earth's First Gods
Pumpkin Sigils & Ritual Smoke
The Hózhó Compass
The Distortus Discipline – Order from Inner Mutation
Witchcraft for the Cold-Blooded Soul
Moonlight Over the Blessingway
Water, Interrupted: When the Body Forgets How to Hold On

Deformed but Divine: Embracing Your Asymmetry

Hexes in the Henhouse: The Farm Witch's Guide to Power

The Reversed Flame: A Grimoire of Inverted Power

Salt, Cells, and Sanity: Reclaiming Balance with Diabetes Insipidus

King of the Broken: Crowning the Flawed Self

Moonlight Scars: Emo Moon Magick and the Art of Lunar Sorrow

Noose Spells: Magick of the Hanging Rope

The Goth Cathedral: Rituals of the Broken and Beautiful

The Cretaceous Codex: Dino Spirits and Fossil Magick

The Turkey Bones Ritual

Nine Lives of Manifestation: Unlocking Bastet's Reality Codes

Chaos Muscles: Building Strength from Twisted Pain

Emo Blood Magick: The Veins of Power

The 3AM Flood: Nighttime Urination, Sleep Loss, and the DI Spiral

The Silence Between the Stars

The Lemon Method: Sour Your Way to Success

Starlit Sovereign

The Rite of Twelve Gates: Walking the Gates of the Duat.

Cornbread and Conjure: Recipes for Riches and Rootwork

The Black Rose Rituals: Emo Love Spells and Obsession Magick

The Eternal Goodbye: Death Magick and Rebirth Rituals

Sinkrot: The Drain That Remembers

The Hybrid Mindset: Thinking Beyond Evolution

Bone Dry: Navigating Dehydration Before It Breaks You

Wreathcraft: Winter Sigils and Yuletide Spells

The Rite of Twelve Mouths

S'mores of the Damned: Haunted Recipes for Halloween Night

Rethink the Drink: A Beverage Survival Guide for DI Warriors

The Shadow Chord: Guitar Magick and Sonic

Malformed Yet Majestic: Leading When You Feel Wrong Inside

The Cursed Diary: Ink-Stained Spells of the Emo Soul

Anxiety Off Switch: Emergency Reset for a Fried Nervous System

The Energy Heist: How to Take Back Your Life from Drainers

Beyond the Bathroom: Rebuilding Your Social Life With DI

Coyote's Gift for Decision Makers

Ghoul-Goo: Spooky S'mores You'll Die For

Echoes in the Mirror: Scrying and Self-Destruction Magick

Thread and Thorn: Stitching Spells from Rural Cloth

The Mogwai Mind: Building Untouchable Wealth from Small Ideas

Be Your Own Guide: Trust Your Inner Compass

Hormones in Chaos: The Endocrine Puzzle of Diabetes Insipidus

ChronoCleanse: Detox Your Biological Timeline

The Limb You Hide Is the One That Saves You

Leaves, Bones, and Whisper Spells

The Dinosaur Mindset: Prehistoric Tactics for Modern Wealth

Clawing Back Control: A Bastet Method for Boundaries and Empowerment

Samhain Codes of the Forgotten

Orange Alchemy: The Autumnal Spellbook

Monster Within, Master Without

The Sigil That Sleeps

Hearthcraft: Yule Hearth Sigils and Winter Warmth Spells

Temple of the Purring Moon: Rituals from Bastet's Lineage

When the Earth Remembers Your Footsteps

Food for Mood: Eat to Heal Depression, Not Just Survive It
Witch of the Kudzu Vine: Southern Pagan Wealth Secrets
The Invisible Diagnosis: Advocating for Yourself With DI
The Coffin's Lullaby: Sleep Magick and Nightmares as Portals
Ashes of the Will: Rituals for Erasing the Self
The Fracture Rite: Shattering the Magickal Core
Funeral Candles: The Art of Emo Flame Magick
The Black Grimoire: A Blank Ritual for Writing in Absence
Phantom Thirst: A Halloween Survival Guide for Diabetes Insipidus
The Hollow Crown: Emo Royalty and Magick of the Outcast King
Sandpainting for the Soul
Falling Into Balance: Using the Extra Hour to Recalibrate Life
100 Southern Superstitions That Still Work
The DI Child: A Parent's Guide to Raising Hydrated, Happy Kids
The Jungle of Shame: Escaping the Hidden Lab of Doubt
The Witch's Toast: S'mores Spells and Creepy Confections
The Hoodoo Pantry: Spells from the Mason Jar
The Immortal Fortune: Secret Wealth Lessons from Captain Jack Harkness
The Specter's Embrace: Magick for Channeling Ghostly Lovers
Grateful Waters: A Thanksgiving Survival Guide for Diabetes Insipidus
The Seizure Gospel
Harvestbind: Autumn Sigils and Samhain Spells
Doctor Who: The Algorithmic Awakening
Silent Nights, Steady Waters: A Christmas Survival Guide for Diabetes Insipidus
The Extra Hour Effect: How One Hour Can Transform Everything

Blade Between the Breaths

Running with the Mountain Shadows

Echoes of the Failed Experiment – Becoming a Living Legacy

Swamp Witches & River Ghosts: Real Southern Hauntings

Cornbread Prophecies: Magical Recipes from a Southern Table

Doctor Who: The Signal in the Star

Bloomcraft: Spring Sigils and Equinox Enchantments

Vanisher: How to Disappear from the Internet Without Losing Your Life

The Ultimate Christmas Cookie Cookbook

The Unbreakable Parent: How to Mentally Survive Raising Kids in a Broken World

Time Debt: How to Reclaim the Hours You Didn't Know You Lost

One Month, One Million: Unconventional Cash Creation Tactics

Doctor Who: The Cyber Conversion Protocol

Black Friday Frenzy: The Art of Finding Hidden Online Deals

The Grimoire Buried Under the Apple Tree

Digital Couponing Masterclass: Your Step-by-Step Guide to Black Friday Savings

The Fire Inside the Flint

Shadows on the Ceiling: The Emo Guide to Astral Magick

The Bone-Eaters Beneath Us

Black Friday Bundle Blueprint: Creating Irresistible Product Packages for Maximum Sales

Thirteen Nights of Unbinding

Doctor Who: Engines of Influence

Pumpkin Spice Alchemy: Recipes of Fire and Frost

When Raptor Met Rexy: Prehistoric Lessons in Wild Romance

Oblivion's Candle: Burn the Path Behind You

Campfire Curses and Chocolate: A Halloween S'mores Grimoire
The Wallet That Wasn't Mine: Breaking Free from Inherited Scarcity
The Cola Zodiac: What Your Fizz Says About Your Fate
Frostfire Fortune: Unlocking Winter's Hidden Prosperity
Signal Jamming: Detox Your Brain from Info Overload
The Dust of the Forgotten Rite
The Golden Cat Sigils: Drawing Power in Bastet's Name
Mud Magick: The Prosperity of Getting Dirty
Savory Spicefall: Beyond the Pumpkin Pie
Pumpkin Spice Apothecary Kitchen
The Pumpkin Spice Economy: Turning Trends into Billions
The Ember Veil: 13 Nights of Fire Magick
Financial Freeze: When Earning Triggers Panic
The Gingerbread Alchemist: Sweet Recipes with a Twist
Biosynth Power: Programming Yourself from Scratch
Echoes from the Talking Circle
Truffle Alchemy: Fungus of Fortune
Spores of Power: The Truffle Witch's Handbook
Doctor Who: The Tower That Speaks
The Mycelium Veil: Truffle Magick Unbound
Broke But Ashamed: Healing the Shame Wound of Debt
The Evergreen Mind: Growth Through Winter Stillness
The Black Veil Truffle Rite
The Voice Beneath Symbols
Witchlight on the Bayou: Swamp Spells for Sovereignty
I Grew Up Poor and Now I Sabotage My Success
The Lantern of Hollow Souls
Shutdown Survival: A Citizen's Guide to Thriving When Government Stops
When Abundance Feels Like a Threat: Healing the Hidden Fears of Enough

The Scarecrow Grimoire
Owls of the October Veil
Candlewax and Curses: A Halloween Spellbook
Excavating the Inner Fossil – Transforming Fossilized Thoughtforms into Tools of Power
The Yule Witch's Spellbook: Magick for the Holiday Season
Haunted Christmas: Ghost Stories for Winter Nights
The Christmas Survival Guide: Thriving Through the Chaos
The Bone Orchard Rites
Haunted Commerce: The Ghost in the Marketplace
When Money Triggers the Inner Child
Silent Night with the Silence: A Christmas Thriller
The Lightning Crown: Living and Leading Through Seizures
TARDIS Tidings: Festive Stories from the Whoniverse
Autumn Reset: Slowing Down Without Falling Behind
The Trillion Dollar Soul: Rewriting the Currency of Reality
Truffle Eclipse Magick
Micro-Manifestations: Quick Magick That Works
5-Minute Rituals for Busy Witches
The Marshmallow Massacre: Halloween Treats with a Sinister Twist
Blood and Blackberry Thorns
Magickal Mornings: Rituals for a Blessed Christmas Day
Embers of the All-Hallows Fire
The Pumpkin Market Collapse
The Hour You Gained: Transforming Time Into Power
The Chamber Must Be Sealed: Mastering the Power of Controlled Access
The Cursed Manuscript of Petosiris
The Festive Hearth: Creating Holiday Traditions
Darkness Rising: Thriving as Nights Grow Longer
Harvesting Time: Turning the Year's End Into Your New Beginning

Petosiris and the 13th Zodiac Key

Wagewound: When Paychecks Become Identity Prisons

Walls That Watch

The Silent Feast: Rituals of Power in the Longest Night

The Distortus Legacy : Becoming a Deformed King in a Perfect World

The Hollow Masks

The Gratitude Furnace: Forging Gold from Thanks

Feast of Inner Gold: Eating for Energy and Enlightenment

Haunted Commerce: The Season of Spending Spirits

Fear Bonds: How Panic Creates Profit

Black Friday E-Commerce Playbook: Sales Tactics to Skyrocket Your Holiday Revenue

Budgeting for Black Friday: A Holiday Savings Planner

Haunting the Harvest Moon

The Warrior's Water: Emergency Preparedness for People With DI

The First Sip of the Year: A New Year's Survival Guide for Diabetes Insipidus

Doctor Who: The Thirteenth Node

The Unseen Struggle: Mental Health, Anxiety, and Chronic Thirst

The Hearth's Hidden Ledger: Counting Energies as Currency

The Gift Alchemist: Turning Any Offering Into Gold

The Papyrus of the Bound Spirit

The Magick of Leftovers: Transmutation in the Fridge

Frost and Fortune: Christmas Wealthcraft for the Modern Magus

Last-Minute Gifts: Creative Ideas on a Budget

10 Secrets to Surviving Holiday Crowds

The Witch's Dow Jones

The Witches' Graveyard Shift

Pumpkin Sigils: Carving Rites for Midnight Power

The Secret Shopper's Black Friday Guide: How to Get Early Access and VIP Deals

Fever in the Foundation

The Neuralyzer Reset: Reprogram Your Morning Routine

Lightning Lessons of the White Painted Woman

The Enchanted Snowflake

The Magic Sip: Surviving Disney Parks with Diabetes Insipidus

The One Who Draws Through You

Santa's Secrets: A Magical Holiday Planner

Silent Bells, Loud Miracles: Self-Help for the Season of Stillness

The Sugar Spell Codex: Confectionary Magick of Christmas

Autumn Hexcraft: Fallen Leaves, Fallen Barriers

Sleep Like a Fortress: Build a Life Where Insomnia Can't Survive

Nowhere Was Ever Home

Christmas Under the Stars: A Celestial Holiday Guide

Rentproof: How to Never Be Evicted Again

Workless: Escape the 9-5 Without Being Broke

The Gilded Gift: A Wealth Altar for Christmas Morning

The Black Friday Grimoire

The Hollowing: Ceremonies of Spiritual Collapse

Doctor Who: The Nameless Signal

Where the Eagle Hides His Courage

The Dwarf Tyrant's Ascent: Claiming Power in a World of Giants

The Currency of the Dead: Trading with Spectral Bankers

The Icebound Witch: Survival and Magick in the Cold

The Emergency Money Mind: Constant Crisis, Zero Calm

Thirst & Roses: A Valentine's Survival Guide for Diabetes Insipidus

Springing Into Clarity: Mastering the Energy Shift of Daylight Saving

Speed of the Nanotyrant: Agile Strategies for Life's Hunt

The 90-Day Reset: A Science-Backed Guide to Reinvent Yourself Before the New Year

The Coil of Thorns

Timegates Unleashed

Dopamine Fasting 2.0: Rewiring Your Brain in a World of Overstimulation

The Nanotyrannus Mutation: Embracing Your Differentiated Form

Unwritten January: How to Use the Blank Page of the Year to Re-Author Your Life

Feast of the Forgotten Spirits: Ancestor Magick for the Holidays

The Burnout Codex: A System for Thriving Beyond Stress

I Don't Deserve to Have Money

When the King Doesn't See You: The Shadow Predator's Guide

The Reset Ritual :A Guide to Shedding Last Year's Weight—Emotional and Physical—by Spring Cleaning Your Soul

Calendar Alchemy: Learn to Bend Time and Productivity around Your Natural Rhythms

The Mirror Contract: A One-Sentence Agreement with Yourself that Unlocks Real Change

The Nile Formula: Sacred Flow for Millionaire Minds

Forward Momentum: Productivity Rituals for the Lost Hour

Harvest Gold: Wealth Magick of Pumpkin Spice Commerce

The Magick of Christmas Lights: Illuminating Holiday Rituals

Cranberry Crown: Royal Self-Worth through Ritual Meals

Petosiris and the Worms of the Feathered Throne

The Evergreen Equation: Self-Help for Sustained Growth

The Rain Will Wash Us Away: Emo Weather Magick
Snowlight Shadows: Magick Under Frozen Stars
Doctor Who: Merger of Empires
The Light Within the Feast: Magickal Wealth of Yuletide Flame
Momentum Machines: Small Habits Designed to Snowball into Unstoppable Forward Motion
Calm Spells: Magickal Solutions for Anxiety Relief
Santa's Final List: The Naughty Never Leave
The Mystic's Guide to Banishing Worry
The Silence Dividend: Turning Quiet Mornings into Compounding Growth All Year
Charmed Stillness: Rituals to Ease the Mind
Blood Spiral Ascension
The Vanishing Heart Invocation
Crystal Calm: Harnessing Stones for Anxiety
The Nano Tyrant Code: Strength in the Small Predator
The Energy Ledger: Accounting Methods for Vitality, Not Just Money
Snowglobe Mindset: Shake Up Your Thoughts, Settle Into Peace
The Weight of the Feather: Anubis's Codes for Soul Balance
Pocket Peppermint Power: Tiny Rituals for Big Holiday Energy
Shadowkeeper of the Golden Jackal: Anubis's Path to Energetic Protection
The Witch's Breath: Anxiety Relief Through Magickal Breathing
The Tiny Ember: Pocket Motivation for Cold Days
Stocking Sorcery: Mini Spells for Holiday Luck and Prosperity
Warm Hands, Steady Heart: Micro Grounding for Winter Anxiety

The Jackal's Lantern: Guide-Lights for Walking the Dark Path

Anubis's Silent Steps: Rituals for Stealth, Peace & Emotional Quiet

The Bonewake Protocol

Extinction-Proof: How to Outlive Trends, Trauma, and Time

The Fourth Doctor: The Eccentric Wanderer

The Second Doctor: Chaos and Charm in the TARDIS (Patrick Troughton, 1966–1969)

The Third Doctor: Earthbound Defender of Time (Jon Pertwee, 1970–1974)

The First Doctor: Genesis of the Time Lord (William Hartnell, 1963–1966)

The Fourth Doctor: The Eccentric Wanderer *(Tom Baker, 1974–1981)*

The Fifth Doctor: Elegance and Empathy (Peter Davison, 1982–1984)

The Sixth Doctor: A Kaleidoscope of Conflict (Colin Baker, 1984–1986)

The Seventh Doctor: The Strategist of Shadows (Sylvester McCoy, 1987–1989)

The Eighth Doctor: A Time Lord's Renaissance (Paul McGann, 1996)

The War Doctor: A Time Lord's Burden (John Hurt, 2013)

The Ninth Doctor: The Healer of Worlds
(Christopher Eccleston, 2005)

The Tenth Doctor: The Lonely Hero (David Tennant, 2005–2010)

The Eleventh Doctor: The Madman in a Box (Matt Smith, 2010–2013)

The Twelfth Doctor: The Rebel with a Cause (Peter Capaldi, 2013–2017)

The Thirteenth Doctor: Breaking the Mold
(Jodie Whittaker, 2017–2022)

The Fourteenth Doctor: A New Beginning (David Tennant, 2022–2023)

The Fifteenth Doctor: Rewriting the Stars

(Ncuti Gatwa, 2023–2025)

Santa's Shortcut to Success: Micro Habits for a Better New Year

The Midnight Cocoa Manifesto: Comfort Rituals for Hard Nights

Why I Can't Save: Trauma Blocks to Financial Planning

Dino Brain, Mega Goals: Rewire Yourself for Savage Success.

Jurassic Profit: Unearth Your Inner Millionaire Fossil

Scales & Softness: Dating with Dino Heart

Carnotaurus Dreams.

Red Willow Thinking.

Reindeer Resilience: How to Keep Going When You're Exhausted

Candlewick Courage: Lighting Strength in Dark Seasons.

Elf-Mode Focus: Fast Attention Fixes for Busy Seasons

Futureproof Feelings: Emotional Skill-Building for Resilience No Matter What the New Year Brings

The 90-Day Rewire: Transform Your Neural Pathways Before Spring Blooms

Jolly Rich: Christmas Micro-Money Magick for Fast Prosperity.

Gingerbread Gratitude: Mini Practices for a Happier Holiday

Trauma-Spending: When Money Becomes a Drug

Goal Skeletons: Build Minimalist Frameworks for Resolutions That Last

The Snarl Strategy: Growling Back at a World That Silenced You

The Hourglass Reset: Reclaiming What the Clock Took

Yule Claw: Dino Rites of Light in the Darkness

Sacred Circles: Grounding Rituals for Anxious Souls

Clockstopper's Gut: Rebuilding the Core of Time

Winterfire Drive: Harness the Cold Season's Stillness to Ignite Deep Motivation

The 5-Minute Productivity Hack: Small Steps to Big Results

Light Ascending: A Self-Help Guide to Longer Days

Inner Economy: Trade Self-Doubt for Confidence Like a High-Value Currency

Simple Success: Decluttering Your Life for Better Results

The Resilient Mind: Thriving in Tough Times

The 2026 Playbook: Mastering the Year Ahead

The Spring Sleep Solution: Conquering Fatigue After Time Change.

The Hormonal Compass: Navigate Back to Your Youth

Golden Vision: Eating for Your Eye Color with the Power of Ghee

Lionhearted Love: Strength in Relationships

MiB Mindset: Think Like a Cosmic Agent

The Ladder of Small Wins: Climb Out of Stagnation by Stacking Micro-Victories

The Momentum Hour: Gaining More in Less Time.

The Year of You: A Self-Help Blueprint for Unapologetic Self-Ownership

The Dust That Watches You Back.

The Astral Parent

Shadow of the King: The Nanotyrannus Parable

Tiny Tidings of Triumph: Small Wins That Change Your Life

Dwarf Tyrant Rising: When You're the One They Overlook

The Bank Account Mirror: Healing How You See Yourself Through Money

Cretaceous Black

When Love Costs Too Much: Romantic Triggers and Financial Wounds

Dream-Eater's Guide to Wealth

Unzipped Reality: The Jacket That Opens Portals
The Power of No: How to Set Boundaries and Get Rich
Keeper of the Desert Veil: Anubis's Teachings on Illusion & Truth
Redacted Stargates: Stories the SGC Buried
The Clock That Dripped Time
Doctor Who: The Silent Acquisition
Hairline Manifestation: Unlocking Power at the Edge of Thought

Get Some Tarot cards: https://www.makeplayingcards.com/sell/apophis-occult-shop

Get some shirts: https://www.bonfire.com/store/apophis-shirt-emporium/

<u>Instagrams:</u>
@apophis_enterprises,
@apophisbookemporium,
@apophisscardshop
Twitter: @apophisenterpr1
Tiktok:@apophisenterprise
Youtube: @sg1fan23477
Hive: @sg1fan23477
CheeLee: @SG1fan23477

Podcast: Apophis Chat Zone: https://open.spotify.com/show/5zXbrCLEV2xzCp8ybrfHsk?si=fb4d4fdbdce44dec

Newsletter: https://apophiss-newsletter-27c897.beehiiv.com/

If you want to support me or see posts of other projects that I have come over to: **buymeacoffee.com/mpetchinskg**

I post there daily several times a day

Get your Dinowicca or Christmas themed digital products, especially Santa Raptor songs and other musics. Here: **https://sg1fan23477.gumroad.com**

Apophis Yuletide Digital has not only digital Christmas items, but it will have all things with Dinowicca as well as other Digital products.

www.ingramcontent.com/pod-product-compliance
Lightning Source LLC
LaVergne TN
LVHW022009200926
848481LV00007B/2309
* 9 7 9 8 3 4 8 1 0 5 7 1 6 *